START A SMALL BUSSINESS ONLINE

Top 10 Ways To Earn Money Online

By

Stephen Nzurum

ISBN: 9798725865332

Disclaimer

The information contained in "**Start a small business online**" is meant to serve as a comprehensive collection of strategies that the author of this eBook has done research about. Summaries, strategies, tips and tricks are only recommendation by the author, and reading this eBook will not guarantee that one's results will exactly mirror the author's results. The author of the eBook has made all reasonable effort to provide current and accurate information for the readers of the eBook. The author and it's associates will not be held liable for any unintentional error or omissions that may be found. The material in the eBook may include information by third parties. Third party materials comprise of opinions expressed by their owners. As such, the author of the eBook does not assume responsibility or liability for any third party material or opinions. Whether because of the progression of the internet, or the unforeseen changes in company policy and editorial submission guidelines, what is stated as fact at the time of this writing may become autdated or inapplicable later.

Contents

Starting a home business can be daunting. Many actions need to be taken and you should do your homework first.

First, you need a place to start, such as another room or at least a room you can book, so it becomes a special place where you have a computer, desk, shelves, filing cabinets, telephone, and modem.

Then evaluate the available time. ie do you start working part-time or do you have the resources to go full time?

When you talk about resources, you should be able to spend some money on resources like the Internet plan you're on, printer and paper, ink cartridges, pens, laptops, diary, files and attachments, and I recommend old-fashioned Teledex to get passwords and store your favorite phone numbers.

I know you can do this on your computer, but you know what happens when an error or power failure occurs,

Can you do it without a home computer? I think you can use an internet cafe or library, but this article is about working from home.

You have now set up a home shopping center. What now?

Investing in a home-based business is good and good, but the best and first investment should be itself. You need some knowledge of how to build an online store, but you also need to develop the right mindset to be willing to skillfully set up your nest and manage it successfully.

Fortunately, it's time to do it. Yes, even 5 years ago it was very difficult to be a newcomer online, because these people were pioneers of today and you can get the knowledge to help you in a big way. But where and how and which one to choose.

Well, here are some tips.

First, research is essential. For beginners it just Google! Yes, you have certainly heard the popular phrase, so "Google" "home business" in the search box and see what appears.

WOW !!! There are hundreds of them! Don't be amazed, just look at a few. see many species out there.

Then decide what type you want to do.

TOP 10 IDEAS OF MAKING MONEY ONLINE

This is the most exciting part of this book.Let me introduce you with Top 10 Idea of making money online that you can consider in order to help you to build additional side income and most importantly financial freedom eventually.

IDEA 01 : Apps or Applications

Apps or applications is another way of making money as a lot of people are uses smart phone and are familiar with Apps. Moreover, developing an app is now easier than ever, though complicated versions become a design team. If you can come up and develop good ideas for apps, you can generate significant revenue every day.

Here are a few tips for developing the iPhone applications in ten simple steps.

- Garner technical knowledge on how to use C++
- Start up by downloading the SDK software's from the apple website itself. If a much more flexible option is needed one can Google over a million SDKs and download it.
- Next up, the user can use the iPhone simulator in order to test the created program

or debug the created application.

- Various other software's are provided by apple in order to optimize the application
- The apple website also has an interface builder to design its applications
- The You Tube website also provides tons of tutorial videos that show how to make such software
- Cocoadevcentral is another application that lets you create your own applications for the iPhone.
- The website for apple iPhone also allows one to make the software and digitally distribute it over to the consumers. This concept of create test and share is really helpful to the people.
- Use a Mac book for the best results in creating applications
- Make sure to check back the applications created in order to remove bugs.

The key lies in this concept. Must be attentive, easy to use and addictive. Games are the most popular types of applications, but they are also more expensive. But if your concept is valid, you can earn a significant amount year after year with a great appeal.

IDEA 02 : Write The Article

There are various websites such as Linkedin, Medium e.t. c that allow you to publish articles on almost every

topic that does not require money or are more than just filling in a simple registration form. In addition, you can subscribe to products from parties interconnected by sources such as Amazon. The more people visit your articles, the more money you can earn from the affiliate products you sell.

But you will have to write many good and interesting articles to attract attention that you must be lucrative. Many of the most successful writers of articles using the above pages earn several hundred to several thousand dollars a month.

This means you have to write at least and maybe more than 100 articles to accomplish these goals. But it's available and does not cost its own money, so it's almost clear to write in these places. As with other passive income ideas, the topic you choose is too wide to reach a large audience that is still close enough to be considered an authority.

How To Write An Article

- Step one: Article Ideas

In order to write, you need an idea, right? So guess what? The best ways to find some is to read topics you are interested in. So lets say you were interested

in sports cars, or more exact, how fast is a Porch? You can find this answer and more in newsletters, articles, forums, and blogs and more.

- Step two: Classifying ideas

So now you have some ideas floating around in your head. You need to classify the ideas into categories and topics. To stay with the Porch idea, different categories would be forums, news articles, blogs, and more. Each of these will have it's own topic that can be written into an article. At the same time you can write down some questions you want answers to. And these can be transformed into an articles.

- Step three: Writing the article

After you have accomplished the first two steps, it's time to write the article! From the first couple of steps you should have some ideas on articles.

A pretty good thing you can start out with is a question you can ask and have the rest of the article to answer it. The body of an article should have anywhere from 2-3 paragraphs This is probably the easiest way on writing and better for the reader, since it won't have just one boring looking article. It better please the reader's eye, if not they won't read it.

If you can, when the article calls for it, use bullet

points, 1,2,3. It's an attention getter and the reader can focus better seeing these.

- Step Four: Formatting your article

Now, every article that is written will always have three elements. And these are:

- Headline
- Body
- Conclusion

Submitting articles is also free. We usually spend money on creating a website.

Today, there are a number of cheaper websites or even free such as Twitter, Medium, facebook. The cost only arises if you improve your strategy using some software. Some people automate their business using software robots or other plug-ins.

If you want to publish your book, it's cheaper to do it online for example you can do it on Amazon. In business, what you really need to invest is your time creating everything and your creativity to create new strategies. Continuous learning is also an advantage.

IDEA 03 : Network marketing

Network marketing is probably one of the most popular ways to earn a passive income. It is an industry that offers customers different products and / or services to pay on an ongoing basis, which in turn creates a passive income.

The disadvantage of network marketing, however, is that, in order to create a passive income that is large enough to live on, often takes many years of hard work. Although the products and services can be good, the lifestyle you are looking for is never possible through this industry alone.

Here are some useful tips on how to get started on online marketing correctly:

1.Before you actually go into online marketing, gather all the necessary resources you will need and learn as much as you can about the business. This is not a difficult task as you can conveniently obtain all that you need from the internet.

2.Create your web marketing plan. This will be your roadmap to your success. Set your goal and work your way to get to your goal and achieve your target earnings. Your plan is your key to all the opportunities that you'll meet along the way.

3.Take full advantage of the internet such as Scentsy,

Advocare, Younique e.t.c . There are several doors of web opportunities you can find from the internet that you wouldn't find elsewhere. The world is practically at your fingertips with the internet.

4.Build your online tools. You can start mostly with the free internet marketing tools plus some powerful paid tools and then steadily upgrade your tools. You must ensure that the tools are useful to get to the network marketing goal you have set.

5.Build your network. The business is still a numbers game. This means, the more contacts and leads you have, the better your chances to convert them to your actual customers from whom you can earn your income.

6.Start to work hard - really hard. This is what's going to buttress your way to success. There are several temptations that may derail you from achieving success in network marketing. But if you are prepared to work hard, there's no stopping you to get what you want.

7.Enjoy what you're doing and always remember to

share your success. You'll find it easier to get to your destination of success when you don't think of it as hard work. Have fun and don't forget to share with others your success.

IDEA 04: Internet Marketing

One of the most recent and profitable forms of establishing significant passive income is through internet marketing. Although this method requires some time in advance to get started and some ongoing support on your part, the amount of revenue that can be generated from this specific system can be much larger than any other business form and probably number one. way to recession-proof your income!

It is important to be prepared to invest in you future, the problem with this is that there is a lot of information and memberships you can buy. Firstly, you need to decide on which form of traffic generation you are going to try first. Some of which are:

- Video Advertising
- Affiliate Marketing
- Social Network Marketing
- Pay Per Click Advertising
- And many more.

For any form of marketing it needs to be done well to be efficient. A badly written ad will not be a wise investment as it wont generate as much traffic.

There are also different 'rules' for each method. For example with forum advertising you need to ensure that you are present and making a contribution to the forum for a certain period of time before you start advertising and providing links to your products or website.

IDEA 05: Stock Photography

Do you like to take a picture? If so, you can generate revenue by uploading your photos to one of the websites of different photo photos like Shutterstock and Dreamstime.

If they are considered good enough, they will appear on these websites where you will earn small revenue for each photo you receive.

This method may take a while and many of your images may not be selected. But this can generate a good profit every month if you build enough inventories. If photography is a passion for you, then this method can work well for you, because it does not require any money and can be built over time.

These are just some of the great passive income ideas you can use to build a healthy income over the years. Remember that the heart of passive income lies in the development of a concept that appeals to enough people and will continue to sell.

- What you need to start selling stock photography?

You need a high-quality digital SLR camera and lenses. There are a lot of cameras in the market with great features but you need a bigger budget for DSLRs.

They are ideal but are expensive. Fortunately, when you're in a tight budget, there are some stock photo agencies that will accept micro-stock photos from digital cameras of at least two to three pixels.

You will also need some kind of software like photoshop, Fotor,Inkscape and Pixlr for making adjustments to your stock photos. You need it to remove imperfections in your photos and to adjust the colors and contrasts in your photos. The well-known software used for editing is Adobe Photoshop. There are a lot of tutorials you can search that will help you improve your editing skills.

- What are the guidelines in stock photography?

There are strict guidelines you need to follow when taking pictures for a stock photography business. In order for your photos to be considered stock photo quality, they need to be modest, properly taken, skilfully exposed and with high resolution.

These photos must be what your customers are looking for. You must be able to have an in-depth understanding of the markets and how and what to shoot. You must also know what images are regularly required but in short supply.

IDEA 06 : Blogging

Blogging is an outstanding way to make money without much stress. once you build your auditorium, keeping your site easy. All you have to do is keep a regular schedule for new content and respond to those who respond.

Many very successful blogs take only one or two hours to work every day, but they can generate tens of thousands of dollars during that time.The goal is to choose the topic or topic that is wide enough to attract a lot of people but close enough to make your blog an authority over the subject.

If you find the right topic that gives a balance between these extremes, you have a strong page for passive income.

1.   What are you reasons for blogging?

You need to decide what you are blogging for. Is it for fun or profit? If you are chasing visitors to your blog, what do you want them to do when they arrive.

2.   Decide what you are going to blog about?

If you are very certain about the reason that you are blogging then that will help you understand and decide on what you are going to blog about. What you are going to blog about is also determined by the people that you are trying to talk to. You can blog about current news, viral videos or controversial topics. You can stick to a certain topic, eg car repairs, or how to get a six pack.

3. Free blog or paid blog?

Free blogs are all over the web, simply do a web search and you can find some. Some examples are blogger.com, WordPress.com, blog.com and Weebly.com. Now with most things in life freedom isn't free. Your blog will not be your own, the domain will be something like bradsblog.wordpress.com so you will have the same domain name as many other people. If you are looking to make money most of the free services don't allow you to advertise on their sites.

Paid blogs -

For a paid blog you have to pay for the domain and the hosting. You will then own the blog yourself and therefore have more control over the blog when you begin to try and make money.A lot of the free blogs

don't allow you to advertise on it. You can use the free program WordPress.org program to put on your blog, which will give you themes and utilities to help make your blog. Cheap options is brainhost.com, HostGator.com, GoDaddy.com all offer hosting solutions. For example: GoDaddy.com hosting starts at $2.99/month. So you are looking at about $36 dollars a year for hosting.

4. Domain names

Now you will have to register a domain name (this is the actual name of your website/blog). Domains start at about $8 but can go up into the thousands. You can use a service at GoDaddy.com or HostGator.com to register you domain name.. The more popular domain names usually cost more.

5. Traffic

When you put something on your blog you want people to read it or watch it. This is where traffic comes in. If you want your blog to be successful you need to learn to get traffic to it.There are many different options here depending on your expertise and budget.

Basically traffic can be broken down into free and paid traffic.

Free traffic includes

- Search engine traffic,
- Social media traffic (Facebook, twitter etc),

PPC (paid per click) advertising, eg the little ads you see at the top of every Google search,

- Solo ads which is where you pay someone with a large list of email subscribers to email them and tell them about your blog,
- Banner advertising - you buy an advertisement space on a website for a set term eg 1 month 6 Days

IDEA 07: Affiliate Marketing

This is probably the most popular form of passive online income. While some may consider it actively in the sense that you are marketing products or services, the truth is that many affiliate marketing sites are naturally passive and provide information such as blogs or special pages that appeal to specific groups of people who again buy the products. Again.

- Steps on How to Start Affiliate Marketing Successfully

An affiliate marketing business does not take too much to get started and the rewards you can reap are great. If you want to know how to start affiliate marketing, there are a few things that you will need.

First you will need a website, or a couple of them if can. You actually do not need to have your own paid personal website; you can use a free blog using Blogger or WordPress. Not all affiliate programs will require you to have a website for you to join, but the big players do and it is their affiliate ID's that will be generally associated with your website.

Eventually you will find that it is better to have a couple of different websites, each one dedicated to particular advertisers and services, but if you're just starting having just one website is enough.

The next step to starting affiliate marketing is to join at least one of the major networks. Although there are many small businesses offering independent affiliate marketing programs, participation in large companies such as Commission Junction or Link Share has several benefits. It is also advisable to join multiple companies and promote their products.

And by joining a large network, it's easier to keep an eye on all your advertising efforts because all your data is aggregated, you can even see sales and payments from a single account. Not to say that independent programs are useless, there are actually many companies offering connected programs over a network and independently at the same time.

Affiliate marketing is the most popular trend today. Ideally, you do not need a large capital to start an online business. Sometimes there is no need for capital because there are some processes that are free. Examples are blogs. Creating a blog is free, but you can use it for your online strategy.

Gradually, retailing is not new to us. But we can make it a new concept if we continue to renew. Online businesses were previously unthinkable. Using effective ideas, someone can create a new world, a new company, a new life, and some new ideas for passive income.

There are several different ways to make money on the internet, but email marketing surpasses the rest.

This is one of the simplest ways to generate passive online income and the best part is that almost anyone with a computer can do it.

The final step to starting affiliate marketing is knowing which companies to avoid. Try to keep your

distance from programs that promise to get you rich quick;

IDEA 08 : Real Estate

Renting your rental property can generate significant passive income. If you have a room you do not use or an apartment, you can rent the tenants interested and earn money. Neither should you be directly involved in this process. Buying real estate for rent is also a good way to create passive income streams.

The monthly rental income created on the basis of one or more housing may add additional income to the household and, in some cases, may replace the current primary sources of income.

Previously, it has been a great way to deal with it, but with the current state of the economy and the general lack of confidence in this arena, it is beginning to fall in popularity and strength.

Cash flow Positive real estate: Passive income can be generated from residential or commercial properties.

Real estate is what most people think of when it comes to passive income. But it is only a passive income when the rent you receive exceeds your mortgage, tax, maintenance and expenses.

Otherwise, your rental home is only a commitment that costs you money - you get no money. If that is the case with you, you probably wonder about making money from the value.

Real Estate investing is one of the easiest ways to make money. In one way, that's true. You don't need a degree of any kind but you do need to educate yourself. With a reasonably small investment and a fair amount of work, you can buy a property and sell it for a healthy profit and the long-term future always pays off in real estate.

The learning curve can be a little steep when just starting out. Real Estate investing, no matter where you live, can seem like a complicated business. Here are some things to consider when getting started.

You'll need to invest in some time before investing your money. Be realistic and think about what financial goals you want to achieve and over what time frame. But remember this... home prices have always been rising and always will be. Like any market though, property prices may go down, and when they do, worried, uneducated owners/investors sell, smart investors buy.Work for a Broker or Become One.

 A lot of brokers start out as being agents and some go straight to the source and become a broker right away.

It all depends on what kinds of certifications you need where you are living. This is one essential thing to consider when you start your real estate career.

The most important thing is to learn the ins and outs of the business through schooling and to take the necessary certification tests. Then, you can work out how you are going to get employment and whether or not you are going to start your own business or become a broker after that.

An average person who has inherited a small home and a plot or an apartment can rent it to generate passive income. Rental income for your apartment can be used to pay a second mortgage. Such a system is for a long-term investment.

Using our properties to generate passive income for a longer investment is a wise decision we can make. Using these resources to earn income can be short-lived, because our wealth favors overtime. Though the value of land value increase is animal of structural maintenance.In addition, tenants can come and go. So you have to be more creative in using your stuff.

You can also convert your property to a fitness center. Sports equipment is slowing down very slowly. Today, many people are crazy about health and fitness.

IDEA 09 : Online e-Commerce Store
Make money driving traffic to your site. Creating an online business is a great source of online revenue and can maximize profits if you know to bring customers into your business. More information on marketing and SEO to find out how to better promote your website.

Automated Completion Sites: Build an ecommerce site that can effectively handle and fill in orders with little involvement to create a passive income.

- How to Improve the Online Visibility of Your E-Commerce Store

If you had an e-commerce site with 200 products and

all the pages, including the homepage and category pages had the same title and meta descriptions then your site is going to perform poorly in search engines.

You can check this by doing a site operator search on Google. For instance go to Google and type in site:www.yoursite.com. If your site suffers from this problem you'll notice that in the results returned all

the pages will have the same or familiar titles and meta descriptions displayed. The listings for each page may look the same and not be uniquely descriptive for each page.

You could also set up a Google Webmaster Tools account. Google will be kind enough to give you HTML suggestions as how to improve your pages and resolve any duplication issues.

Make sure you site has a clear hierarchical structure. Pages shouldn't be buried so deep down the structure that they are hard to get to both for search engines and users. One of the best structures for an e-commerce site is a pyramid structure.

IDEA 10 : Create an ONLINE COURSE
Selling online courses is one of the best passive income ideas in 2020. We still see huge sales growth

for course makers. If you decide to sell a course on your website or on a platform like Udemy, you will find clients who want to learn your inner tips and tricks.

If you have followed two types and have built your audience, selling the course to your site can help you determine how much passive income you earn. Finding your customers is up to you.

It will be a bit easier if sold on course platforms like Udemy, but your courses can be discounted over time. This affects the number of passive earnings you earn.

You need to decide on the course you will be selling for people to benefit from it. There are different kinds of courses such as :

- Game courses
- Programming courses
- Youtube video courses
- Marketing
- And many more

So you need to choose which course you want to based on or make research on what people need to know about and make courses on it.

Conclusion

Making money online is actually money that comes to you every day without you having to make any physical effort to earn it. Passive income flows to you, whether you do something for it or not. Now it's easy money or what?

Even better, small bussiness is usually associated with inflation in a certain way, so the association usually keeps it rising. In my opinion, passive income is one of the easiest ways to earn extra money you will ever find. When you understand the concept of small business and know how to get your share of these easy money, you are well on your way to achieving financial freedom.

Imagine this. If you can no longer go to work the next morning, how long will you survive without your active income? What is the actual number of years you want to survive if you stop working? That's the goal of your wealth! Imagine being able to wake up every day without having to do anything; You have more income than you had the day before. You wake

up every day and your income has grown. Easy
money, which good result!